HAPPY
Easter!!
April 16, 1995

With love

from

Mom.

to

Kayla

LITTLE ☆ STARS™

SCORPIO

A parent's guide to the little star of the family

JOHN ASTROP

with illustrations by the author

E L E M E N T

Shaftesbury, Dorset ● Rockport, Massachusetts
Brisbane, Queensland

© John Astrop 1994

Published in Great Britain in 1994 by
Element Books Ltd.
Longmead, Shaftesbury, Dorset

Published in the USA in 1994 by
Element, Inc.
42 Broadway, Rockport, MA 01966

Published in Australia in 1994 by
Element Books Ltd.
for Jacaranda Wiley Ltd.
33 Park Road, Milton, Brisbane, 4064

Printed and bound in Great Britain by
BPC Paulton Books Ltd.

British Library Cataloguing in Publication
data available

Library of Congress Cataloguing in publication
data available

ISBN 1-85230-544-4

CONTENTS

THE TWELVE SIGNS

Everyone knows a little about the twelve sun signs. It's the easiest way to approach real astrology without going to the trouble of casting up a chart for the exact time of birth. You won't learn everything about a person with the sun sign but you'll know a lot more than if you just use observation and guesswork The sun is in roughly the same sign and degree of the zodiac at the same time every year. It's a nice astronomical event that doesn't need calculating. So if you're born between

May 22 and June 21 you'll be pretty sure you're a Gemini; between June 22 and July 23 then you're a Cancer and so on. Many people say how can you divide the human race into twelve sections and are there only twelve different types. Well for a start most people make assessments and judgements on their fellow humans with far smaller groups than that. Rich and poor, educated and non-educated, town girl, country boy, etc. Even with these very simple pigeon holes we can combine to make 'Rich educated town boy' and 'poor non-educated country girl'. We try to get as much information as we can about the others that we make relationships with through life. Astrology as a way of describing and understanding others is unsurpassed. Take the traditional meaning of the twelve signs:

Aries - is self-assertive, brave, energetic and pioneering.

Taurus - is careful, possessive, values material things, is able to build and make things grow.

Gemini - is bright-minded, curious, communicative and versatile.

Cancer - is sensitive, family orientated, protective and caring.

Leo - is creative, dramatic, a leader, showy and generous.

Virgo - is organised, critical, perfectionist and practical.

Libra - is balanced, diplomatic, harmonious, sociable, and likes beautiful things.

Scorpio - is strong-willed, magnetic, powerful, extreme, determined and recuperative.

Sagittarius - is adventurous, philosophical, far-thinking, blunt, truth-seeking.

Capricorn - is cautious, responsible, patient, persistent and ambitious.

Aquarius - is rebellious, unorthodox, humanitarian, idealistic, a fighter of good causes.

Pisces - is sensitive, imaginative, caring, visionary and sacrificing.

If you can find anyone in your circle of friends and acquaintances who isn't described pretty neatly by one of the above it would be surprising. Put the twelve signs into different lives and occupations and you see how it works. A Taurean priest would be more likely to devote his life to looking after the physical and material needs of his church members, feeding the poor, setting up charities. A Virgoan bank robber would plan meticulously and never commit spontaneous crimes. A Leo teacher would make learning an entertainment and a pleasure for her pupils.

So with parents and children. A Capricorn child handles the business of growing up and learning in a very different way to a Libran child. A Scorpio parent manages the family quite differently to an Aquarian. The old boast, 'I'm very fair, I treat all my children the same', may not be the best way to help your little ones at all. Our individual drive is the key to making a success of life. The time when we need the most acceptance of the way we are is in childhood. As a parent it's good to know the ways in which our little ones are like us but we must never forget the ways in which they are different.

LITTLE SCORPIO

Little Scorpios are a puzzle. You may be welcoming into the family a little angel or a little demon. One thing is certain; bouncy tough little boy or sweet cuddly little girl, this is no middle of the road babe. Scorpios seem to be in this world in order to try out the absolute extremes of human possibilities. A great responsibility for such a little one. Maybe that's why he or she looks just that little bit more serious than all the other babes.

Scorpios are intense; that sounds a tough word for a child but you better believe it. Everything that they do, they do with passion or they don't do it at all. Deeply emotional, they tune in to the rest of the family ups and downs as if they were an encephalograph wired in to everyone's head. Not only do they take in everything, they seem to have the strength to deal with the stress of the most traumatic of family rows and take it in their stride. You will soon become aware of a great strength of will in little Scorpio, never accepting defeat in any project no matter how difficult or overawing. In fact, for this little battler, no project is really worth entertaining unless it is difficult. You'll bite your lip trying to stop pointing out

that there's an easier way. No use, where's the appeal for a Scorpio in the easy way. Scorpios, like  the other water signs, Cancer and Pisces, share a strong emotional response to life but unlike the other two, may often see it as a weakness to allow expression of these strong feelings. For this reason these characters often bottle up emotions to be released in an explosive outburst out of all proportion to the seemingly trivial cause. Scorpios are secretive. Part of the Scorpio's survival instinct makes for this secrecy and the ability to ferret out everybody's secrets whilst keeping their own a closed book is the most infuriating Scorpionic talent. There'll be no skeletons in the closet in your family with a small Scorpio around to ferret them out. These little characters spend most of their lives acting the private eye, looking for clues, 'sussing' out people and solving tricky problems. They are great games players if a modicum of strategy is involved. Quite a few of the world's greatest chess grandmasters and more than a few generals were little Scorpios. Passionate in their loyalty to friends, woe betide the person who crosses a Scorpion. The dreaded sting in the tail is no fairy tale. Even the tiniest Scorpio will deeply internalise a hurt, let it smoulder around for a while and then seek revenge well out of proportion to the original hurt. When it comes to battles Scorpios never fight fair. Their uncanny awareness of everybody's weak spots gives them a head start in any confrontation. They hurt! Don't fight 'em, love 'em. If you get close to a Scorpio you've the most devoted loving companion that you'll ever find and heaven help anyone that tries to harm you. As pals and protectors they're unbeatable.

The Baby

The Scorpio babe will let you know in no un-
certain terms when you're getting things wrong.
There's no way you'll stop this one howling with a
cuddle if it's a drink that's required. Somewhat like
little Taurus in requiring time before moving on
to the next stage of development, there is no way
this one will be pushed into a new experience or

experiment with a strange
but tasty food item before
they're ready. Unlike other
more active babes little
Scorpio will gaze fixedly at
their fluffy toys, beads and
mobiles as if taking in the

very essence of their being. This is when you'll
notice the deep penetrating eyes that follow your
every movement around the room. Don't try star-
ing him out, your eyes'll water and you'll get a

funny feeling that it's not a baby looking at you! Scorpio babes start as they mean to go on, understanding things. Highly alert if not the most active of little souls, everything and anything within reach is explored and thought about and filed away in that clever little mind for later use. Once bathtime is added to the repertoire and deemed pleasurable it can become this little water sign's passion, even provoking rare leg and arm flailing splashing sessions. Little Scorpios usually carry on to enjoy swimming all their lives.

THE FIRST THREE YEARS

Once your small Scorpion is up on two sturdy little pins the games start. Your apparently childproof home suddenly seems to be full of the most dangerous temptations for your little, super problem-solving mini Captain Daring. Scorpions have to try to overcome difficulties even at that early age. If you've hidden the best glass vase on top of the cupboard out of harm's way, how did it suddenly appear with little Scorpio making a flour and water milk shake on the kitchen floor? The joke is that if you hadn't made it so temptingly unreachable it wouldn't have appealed anyway. This could be a clue to handling little Scorpio's desire to go to extremes. If you want to get them into action with something make it difficult or at least not too readily available. This babe may hang on to the comfort of the warm wet nappies a little longer than you'd hope but Scorpios apply their own system of discipline and the transition to potty trained can happen quite suddenly when you're beginning to despair. Great interest will be shown in the life around, nothing escapes comment and questions – pregnant ladies, other babies, people kissing, dogs peeing, cats hunting. It's as if they have to pack in a lifetime of experience in the first few years. At around two to three years strong attachments will be made with just one or two quite fastidiously chosen little friends, usually with your little one being the dominant half of the relationship. Even at this stage you can see they will be quite protective of any little friend. Little Scorpio is highly imaginative and despite an early quite mature understanding of the real world is able to concoct wild scenarios in play that are a delight to listen to.

THE KINDERGARTEN

Surprisingly enough, for all the challenging and competitive nature of little Scorpio you'll probably find that it's the role of observer that is taken rather than joining in all the active play of the nursery school. Toying halfheartedly with a few crayons your little one will be acutely aware of everything that is going on, sorting out her place in the rankings. If you can prise a word out of her at the end of the session you find out who likes who, who hurt who, who's Mummy's got what, who's Daddy doesn't live at home. Even at this stage people will matter more than games and toys

and in a modest way little Scorpio will step in and set little differences to rights, bossing the others around if they stray from the rules of whatever games they are playing. Your little Scorpio seems to be blessed with a magnetic and compulsive will that little contemporaries will not argue against and generally will be popular in the class.

SCHOOL AND ONWARDS

In the boisterous hurly burly of the first school years little Scorpio may become somewhat withdrawn. The love of privacy will keep his friends few but well chosen. Although most little Scorpios find school work relatively easy they are subject to strong emotional reactions to the everyday loves and crazes and hurts that children impose on each other. There may be a need to help your small scholar feel okay about letting out feelings at the end of an overwhelming

day. Fanatically loyal to closest friends, the little Scorpion can be quite jealous when their buddies go off with others that they have designated as unworthy. 'Why does Tom want to play with daft ol' Jeremy?' Deep hurts are kept to themselves but beware the unexpected Scorpio revenge on a classmate that has stepped well out of line. Rarely forgiving for any injustice against themselves or their loved ones, little Scorpios retaliate when it's least expected and a little harder than one would think fair. Schoolwork will be worked at in bursts, usually leaving everything to the last minute and then finishing successfully in half the time that should have been allocated to the work.

THE THREE DIFFERENT
TYPES OF SCORPIO

THE DECANATES

Astrology traditionally divides each of the signs into three equal parts of ten degrees called the decanates. These give a slightly different quality to the sign depending on whether the child is born in the first, second or third ten days of the thirty-day period when one is in a sign. Each third is ruled by one of the three signs in the same element. Scorpio is a Water sign and the three Water signs are Scorpio, Pisces and Cancer. The nature of Water signs is basically emotional and responsive so the following three types each has a different way of expressing their responsive natures.

First Decanate - Oct 24 to Nov 2

This is the part of Scorpio that is most typical of the sign qualities. Scorpios are persuaders. Their strong magnetic quality attracts followers and always puts them in a leading position. There is a fanaticism and almost evangelistic attitude to their work that seeks to change others' views to match their own powerful enthusiasms. Nothing is entered into half-heartedly and when a challenge is overcome and has reached its fulfilment it is no longer of interest and is dropped immediately in order to make way for the next. For this reason they often leave their devoted followers behind still dealing with the last enthusiasm, when they themselves have moved on to something quite different. The drastic changes of Picasso's painting from the Blue period to Cubism to Classicism and so on, changed the whole face of modern art but left many followers still clinging to the earlier phases. Escoffier made food an art, Charles Atlas sold a generation on the idea of body building, Dylan Thomas made good poetry accessible and John Cleese put fanatical humour on the map.

Second Decanate - Nov 3 to Nov 12

This is the Imaginative Persuader. This decanate has all the power of the Scorpio combined with the ultra-sensitive imagination of Pisces. The driving force is an understanding of others' feelings and reactions. The Scorpio's ability to discover the deepest secrets of people added to the Piscean's almost psychic awareness of the thoughts and desires of the masses make this part of Scorpio the most publicly persuasive. Billy Graham is only one of many great evangelists who were born in this sign though some of them were not devoted to quite such good causes, as in the case of Joseph Goebbels and his propaganda for the Nazis. Sun Yat-Sen was known as the father of republican China and changed the course of its history. This ability to be able to get inside the needs, desires and feelings of the people makes persuasive and powerful writers and actors in the dramatic field. Often famous characters from this part of Scorpio are subject to scandal or a loss of popularity at the height of their success. General George Patton became for some an embarrassment at the end of WWII.

Third Decanate - Nov 13 to Nov 22

The Responsive Persuader. The combination of the strong protective aspect of the Moon and Cancer combine with Scorpio in this decanate. This gives powerful family ties and a paternal or maternalistic attitude to those with whom these Scorpios share their extreme lives. Often these are the mainstay and organiser of the traditional family gatherings. Frequently those from this decanate inherit or take over a role that has been well established before. In some instances the family business is carried on or traditional family occupations are pursued. Surprisingly there are many great leaders and generals born in this part of the sign but obviously their natural protective instinct is an important advantage to their strategy. The two opposing Field Marshals in WWII, Montgomery and Rommel, had birthdays two days apart! There are strong links with the past and a desire to maintain the best of traditions. Prince Charles has caused some controversy in recent years presenting himself as a strong advocate for maintaining the architecture and values of earlier periods in preference to recent innovations.

OTHER LITTLE SCORPIOS

Mums and Dads like you delighted in bringing up the following little persuaders. Yours will probably turn out to be even more famous!

First Decanate Scorpio

Captain Cook, Marie Antoinette, Benvenuto Cellini, Daniel Boone, James Boswell, Auguste Escoffier, Theodore Roosevelt, Pablo Picasso, Alexander Alekhine, Dr Jonas Salk, Charles Atlas, Barbara Bel Geddes, Dylan Thomas, John Cleese, Joan Plowright, Dick Francis, Helen Reddy.

Second Decanate Scorpio

Edmund Halley, Madame Marie Curie, Fyodor Dostoyevsky, Sun Yat-Sen, General George Patton, John Phillip Sousa, Billy Graham, Joan Sutherland, Katherine Hepburn, Carl Sagan, Demi Moore, Charles Bronson, Whoopi Goldberg, Tatum O'Neal, Jonathan Winters, Roseanne Barr.

Third Decanate Scorpio

Voltaire, Robert Louis Stevenson, Claude Monet, Aaron Copland, Indira Ghandi, Charles de Gaulle, Field Marshall Rommel, Field Marshall Montgomery, Colman Hawkins, Rock Hudson, Calvin Klein, Goldie Hawn, Billie Jean King, Prince Charles, Jamie Lee Curtis, Terry Gilliam.

And Now the
Parents

THE ARIES PARENT

The good news!

The Aries parent may never discover that such powerful and actively strong characters as little Scorpios can be extremely emotionally vulnerable. They tap in to other people's thoughts and feelings almost telepathically, rarely giving away their own. The honest, straightforward Aries 'if you feel it, you show it' attitude can go a long way in helping little Scorpio to share bottled up hopes and fears confidently. They will be united by a love of challenges. Rarely childishly carefree, young Scorpio thrives on deep, passionate interests, and loves converting others to the same cause. The Aries parents will support enthusiastically when necessary but never intrusively, for their own strong  self-reliance makes them respect and encourage their small Scorpio's early development. These little characters rarely accept domineering authority; like Aries, the little Scorpio is a warrior by nature and any dogmatic approach with regard to matters of discipline will be a challenge to be resisted and overcome. Where behaviour is concerned these small powerhouses prefer to shake off bad habits with their own strict brand of self-discipline. They share your Arian need to push everything to the limit but whereas you do it in the name of discovery, little Scorpio goes to extremes to test him or herself. This can manifest as your little one getting up at the crack of dawn every morning and taking a cold shower or laying like a slob in bed until you're forced to drag him out. One thing is certain, nothing lasts forever with your little partner and what seemed like an irreversible habit can be switched off and a fresh start made at the drop of a hat. If you compete with each other in gamesplaying you'll be surprised how quickly little Scorpio gets the subtlety of complicated games such as chess and Scrabble and beats you into second place! Quite a few chess grandmasters are November born.

...and now the bad news!

There will be times when all that Aries and Scorpio power gets the better of you. Both of your signs are ruled by the planet Mars and although positively it can produce some of the most heroic characters amongst the twelve signs, it is negatively the raw material for bullies and dictators. If the two of you start battling against each other the rules are thrown to the winds. Aries can go too far, too quickly, without thinking and little Scorpio, always sensing where an opponent is most vulnerable, goes for it and hurts. The Scorpio sting is not a pleasant thing. If you win just because you're bigger and stronger, then hurt pride can produce sly, secretive disobedience and brooding resentment. You two warriors have to battle from time to time but make sure you're on the same side, this way you'll have the closest, most powerful loving partnership in the whole zodiac.

THE TAURUS PARENT

The good news!

You are affectionate, firm but reasonable, and above all consistent. The powerful young Scorpio, so easily given to extremes of action, will learn with you how to manage and control with some discretion the need to go to the excesses that can typify the Scorpio character. Quick to learn, and highly intuitive, little Scorpios seem irresistibly drawn to the difficult rather than the easy, as if only that is a worthy challenge to their powers. The Taurean parent is usually a stickler for getting the everyday routine jobs out of the way before tackling bigger, more demanding projects. Junior's nature may resist or be totally indifferent to such 'trivialities', until they accumulate and become a Herculean task to be conquered. Let's face it, this little one's room just won't get tidied up until the walls and doors are bursting at the seams and then everything gets the cleaning of its life or even more Scorpionic - gets dumped! All Scorpios, no matter how tiny, need this periodic cleansing and a fresh start back to basics. They

almost psychically sense and respond to other people's thoughts and feelings, making them close, warm and loving companions. If you're feeling down, they'll know almost before you do, and respond comfortingly if not inspiringly, making you feel a whole lot better for just having such a caring little sidekick. You like good solid logic and down-to-earth thinking. Scorpio's bright mind will appreciate discussions on what might seem to you to be very advanced and deep subjects for such tender years. Don't try and skip them though, as she needs to know the answers to life's serious questions and with her natural detective abilities will find them out anyway. Nicer if they can be shared with you.

...and now the bad news!

It is wise to remember that Taurus and Scorpio are opposite signs in the zodiac and can in tense situations become an intolerable pair for the rest of the family. You can be stubborn just for the sake of it and little Scorpios won't let anything or anyone beat them when they feel so inclined. This means that battles between the two of you can seem like sieges and go on just a little too long for comfort. Dogmatic Taurean nagging, without just and logical reasoning, will produce deep and brooding resentment that results in cold, destructive retaliation. Respect the intense power of the little Scorpion and be firm but flexible and you'll have a respectful, eternally loyal friend and never feel the sharp sting in the tail.

♊

THE GEMINI PARENT

The good news!

Your natural Geminean curiosity will delight in studying the probing, penetrating mind of little Scorpio. Though often difficult to understand and rarely as freely expressive as this chatty parent, the little Scorpion will learn quickly from Gemini's stimulating company. Scorpios' 'knowing' minds easily grasp ideas and methods with an ability sometimes far beyond their years. Few secrets are safe from the piercing intuition of this child, who often gives the disconcerting impression of knowing what you are thinking before you have said it. The Gemini parent's fund of knowledge and broad interests will expand and help develop Scorpio's strong self-reliance. Little Scorpio's enthusiasm is all or nothing, black or white but never grey. The need to try everything out is not unlike Gemini's own, but some subtle help from this quick-thinking parent can modify the attractions of the undesirable (which will always be on the agenda!). Whereas you can try something out for size and drop it the moment you know what it's all about, little Scorpio just has to take things about as far as they can go and then a little more. If it's a

new hobby then it will be all pervading and everybody's got to be interested. If it's a new food craze then get in a crate of the stuff and don't worry, it'll be dropped when little Scorpio thinks enough is enough and not until! Sounds like a handful, but the loyalty, strength of character and determination that grows with imaginative and caring companionship, makes the adventure worthwhile. Even a probing Geminean like you is never going to know what really goes on inside the mind of this little companion but keep the information and the stimulation going and there'll never be a dull moment.

...and now the bad news!

For all their self-reliance and seeming independence little Scorpios are emotionally vulnerable. The Gemini nature is hot on communications and will talk things over in order to solve any problem.

Great if you're talking to a like-minded Libran or an Aquarian but it won't always work with little Scorpios. Because their minds are so alert you'd think they'd respond best to a quick bit of logic whenever problems occur. Sorry - you're wrong! They gotta have the hugs and the cuddles and the logic can take a back seat. The Gemini quick switch of moods can be read by little Scorpio as disinterest and to this passionate soul that is the end of the world. Scorpio emotions run deep and need coaxing to find expression, so enjoy the coming together of two good minds but never forget the pleasure of crying on each other's shoulders.

THE CANCER PARENT

The good news!

This has the potential of being one of the best relationships in the zodiac. You're both water signs and experience life in much the same way through the emotions. The Scorpio child will respond well to the demonstrative, caring ways of the Cancerian parent. Young Scorpio senses immediately the genuine feelings of others and reacts accordingly. Like Aries children, Scorpios need a worthwhile challenge to bring out their best; they seem almost to turn the simplest task into a near disaster in order to surmount the difficulty. Cancer will quickly sense this need, understanding that by always testing their extreme potential, Scorpios learn to handle their powerful emotions with confidence. Cancer will realize that a heavy, authoritative manner achieves little with young Scorpio whose inclination for self-discipline is strong. This little powerhouse does nothing by halves and moves from one extreme to the other. You will feel all too often that the old rhyme of the little girl with the curl, 'when she was good she was very very good but when she was bad she was horrid', fits

your small Scorpion very well. Only a doting Cancer Mom or Dad could love both the little saint and the sinner equally! Lucky Scorpio! Anyway, this little wonder makes up for everything by sheer spirit and determination, achieving results in and out of school of which any parent would be proud. Both of you enjoy the home comforts and need little excuse to become 'stay-at-homes' so you may, even if it's only for the sake of little Scorpio, need to get out and about a little more in order to expand your small one's experience of the big bad world outside. Keep it full of fun and adventure!

...and now the bad news!

Almost everything in your relationship will be accompanied with loving hugs so battles will be rare but the obvious clash for you both is when the Cancerian overprotective instincts leave no room for Scorpio's strong self-reliance. This can result in open rebellion but is far more likely to manifest as secretive withdrawal, all communications on that subject being broken off. Hard as it may turn out to be, don't protect little Scorpios; bite your lip, admire their undoubted talent for survival and let them protect you. Whatever you were protecting them from they'll do when you're not around so you're wasting your time. If it's a bad habit you want to break, best use the old Crab's sidestep and get them into positive action by suggesting you understand how impossible it would be to give it up. Then stand back!

♌

THE LEO PARENT

The good news!

When you, the Leo parent, who loves to rule the roost (usually making an excellent job of it), is confronted with the iron will of a little Scorpio, sparks can fly. Head-on confrontations must be avoided at all costs in this relationship. Both have fixed opinions, like their own way, and tend to dig their heels in, but Leo will realise sooner or later that when it comes to sheer grit, tiny Scorpio may surprisingly have the edge. Leos' natural tendency to direct their children can help the intense little

Scorpio to channel the great willpower that can lead to strength or downfall. In understanding the Scorpio child's uncanny talent for psychology (having one's weaker motives 'sussed' is an occupational hazard with parents of little Scorpios) Leo will do well to behave with scrupulous honesty and candour. Nevertheless these two signs have a great deal in common. Both are loyal and warm-hearted,

both have sticking power when it comes to achieving a goal. The Leo parent loves a winner and should derive great satisfaction from young Scorpio's determination to make a success of life. By introducing a little fun and laughter into the 'winning game' to which Scorpio is compulsively drawn, Leo can lighten the intensity of the little water sign, teaching leadership rather than conquest. There is an impulsive quality about Leo that can be somewhat disconcerting for little Scorpio, who likes to feel in control. Big shifts in routine will not be welcomed if it means an obligation to perform for you, the ambitious parent. Little Scorpio's way is to hear all, see all, and say little, and only then when she's good and ready.

...and now the bad news!

Leos are generally the life and soul of the party and if your busy social schedule overlooks one little party at home there could be problems. Scorpio emotions run deep, little injustices are felt strongly and build resentment. There is only one way for a neglected Scorpio to react and that is by going to extremes. They can hold in feelings just so long as the safety valve holds and then blam! Even your loving little babe can hit you where it hurts, below the belt. The Scorpio sting is painful even to the tough old Lion; don't risk it when plenty of warm Leo sunshine can make it redundant.

THE VIRGO PARENT

The good news!

Mentally bright and verbally expansive, you Virgoan parents may find little Scorpio's sometimes impenetrable intensity more than a mystery. Virgos put all the facts on the table, add them up, and come to a correct and well-reasoned conclusion. Little Scorpios rarely put the facts on the table. Secretive but not deceptive, these tiny psychologists intuitively probe surroundings, relationships, experiences, other people, and you, revealing nothing until the appropriate moment.

In this way the little Scorpion builds the self-confidence and strength to tackle life's biggest challenges. The orderly Virgoan needs things to run efficiently and is firm in adhering to a good well-proven system. This is just the kind of strength that young Scorpio respects; the natural instinct to occasionally knock against authority is usually a need to assess its strength and prove that respect is justified. Standing firm, and backed with good friendly Virgoan logic, makes the point clearly to this challenging little character. The Scorpio drive to put everything to the test applies

equally to themselves at both extremes. Working with phenomenal passion on impossible projects on the one hand and lounging around for days in self-indulgent lethargy on the other, they try the lot. If the calm Virgo parent can accept the extremes, and put up more worthy challenges when the 'experiments' look unproductive, Junior's achievements will be a just reward. Although you'll both connect well on mental matters, your Virgoan nature may need a reminder that this small, seemingly independent powerhouse needs lots of loving hugs and emotional reassurance to keep all on a smooth and happy level.

...and now the bad news!

You're a bit of a perfectionist and always want the best for your little one. Only one way to do that: tell him when he gets it wrong, point out where little Scorpio could improve, list the mistakes. Good traditional, self-improving Virgo stuff but, oh no, not the way to handle the little Scorpion. Nagging produces quite the opposite effect to the one desired. If you want little Scorpio to opt out, become outwardly deadpan but inside a seething mass of emotional resentment, then fail to recognise her great achievement in finishing a pretty daunting project and point out a few faults that you happened to spot. Point taken?

♎

THE LIBRA PARENT

The good news!

Whereas you, if you're a typically Libran parent, like the balance of the middle road in all things, the young Scorpio is almost entirely interested in experimenting with extremes. Working with passion, lazing lethargically; warm and loving, cold and cruel; a paragon of good behaviour or positively delinquent, little Scorpions uncontrolled will try them all on for size. These powerful small characters almost demand a strong parent to look up to. Though rarely seeing themselves in this role the easy-going Libran parent has a fair-mindedness which, coupled with a few strong guidelines, will soon gain the respect of little Scorpio. The small Scorpion's penetrating mind grasps things quickly and given sufficient challenge will tackle the most difficult tasks with unbounded enthusiasm. Deeply emotional, although often outwardly calm, the little Scorpion responds warmly to Libran shows of affection. Often creative with a natural good taste (Picasso was a little Scorpio), your little companion will share your love of beauty and artistic

matters. You can help to develop this talent with trips to museums and galleries and plenty of good stimulation in the form of books and mental games. Your love of company and entertaining will be helpful to little Scorpio who, left to his or her own devices, could be a bit of a loner and a stay-at-home. It is strange that these little characters, who show so much self-reliance at such an early age, still often remain painfully shy if they don't get the required help at the right time. There is an underlying seriousness with your little Scorpio that can become quite inward looking if overlooked, and allowed to go to extremes. You should have no real difficulty in injecting regular doses of good-humoured fun, teaching your little one that even playing the fool can bring people closer.

...and now the bad news

Though Libran households rarely indulge in battles or clashes, troubles can occur through the very diplomacy that keeps the peace. Always seeing the other side of the argument can make the harmony-loving Libran a little on the weak side when it comes to laying down the law and sticking to it. If you fail to establish good definite limits on behaviour the challenge in finding just how far it is possible to go may be irresistible for your little Scorpion. The old adage 'you have to be cruel to be kind' may be a little over the top for you but try replacing it with ' you have to be firm to be fair' and see how that works!

THE SCORPIO PARENT

The good news!

The sheer energy of you two Mars-powered superbeings will leave the rest of the family exhausted. You will enthuse and encourage your cute little clone to great heights and tiny Scorpio will respond to the challenge like a Hercules cleaning the Augean stables. Well, maybe not quite so extreme as that but challenge will be the name of the game with you both. Young Scorpios can learn easily from this parent how to develop and deal with the great power this sign manifests. Big Scorpio can give loving support, understanding the intense feelings that lie hidden beneath the deceptively calm surface of this little volcano. All or nothing is the watchword of you both and as comrades in arms you are invincible. This sounds like a militaristic duo but in truth the love of battle and challenge is Scorpio's driving force. Intelligent, perceptive, little Scorpio learns quickly and easily, though he or she may often neglect the more mundane necessities in favour of more demanding projects. Both highly intuitive, born psychologists, parent and child will enjoy discussing others about them, discovering their strengths and their weaknesses. If any couple can dish the dirt in the

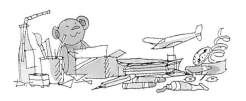

privacy of their own home it is this one! That is, of course, where other people are concerned. When it comes to letting on exactly how they feel themselves, Scorpions are firmly placed near the bottom of the league. It's not really insecurity that does this but more the Scorpio's deadly weapon. Invulnerability! If you don't know where I can be hurt you can't get me. Don't do this one to each other; if you can't trust another Scorpio who can you trust. Tell all! A strong Scorpio parent is one of the few who could actually overawe this child, so while you're being this great role model don't forget to let your hair down now and again to allow Junior to see that you're just an ordinary superhero like him.

...and now the bad news!

Intense understanding makes you the most loyal of friends and the most devastating of enemies.

Mutual respect should keep the power struggles to a minimum, but confrontation of two Scorpios can seem like a fight to the death, each capable of inflicting unhealable hurt on the other. Campaign on the same side and you can conquer the world. Better still, fight out your battles on a chessboard. This must be the supreme Scorpio game (if she does this then I'll do that and then she'll move here and I'll move there and then I've got her, yes, real Scorpio stuff, chess).

THE SAGITTARIUS PARENT

The good news!

Your Sagittarian nature will always see your little Scorpio as a friend that's just a little bit smaller than the others. You couldn't be a stuffy old parent if you tried, life is too great an adventure for you to fall into that trap. Sagittarian parents admire independence and treat their children, no matter how tiny, with frank honesty and respect. Little Scorpio's strong will, independence and positive manner offers no threats to the Archer's great love of freedom. Sagittarians like to keep on the move but little (and big!) Scorpios can sometimes be somewhat 'stick in the mud' if left to their own devices. No chance of that with you around and once you've experienced the first resistance at hauling little Scorpio off on an unplanned trip you'll learn next time how to make it an attractive challenge that needs to be beaten. The powerful young Scorpion needs a strong parental figure to live up to and Sagittarius's friendly straight-talking nature fits the bill well. No sticklers for dull routine, these parents take life as a continuing adventure and the resulting day-to-day surprises and challenges can become, with a little subtle cajoling, the stuff of life to little Scorpio. Between the two of you, a few

THE CAPRICORN PARENT

The good news!

You have all the patience in the world and are well organised and capable where running a home is concerned. One thing you must have though is a smooth-running system that you can stick to come what may. Powerful little Scorpios won't have to go to extremes with this parent to establish just how far they can go. Good, firm but fair guidelines will be set and adhered to, long before Junior begins to get the hang of rebelling. Capricorn, as with everything else, steps into the responsibility of parenthood with eyes wide open and plans well made. Ambitious for their children, they know that a good predictable pattern makes family life run smoothly and builds confidence in their young ones. Though with little Scorpios one must expect a few battles, these will be more for the experiment of testing their own strong wills than an attack on authority. Potentially the most powerful sign in the zodiac, Scorpio admires strength and will need great help and reassurance in dealing with this explosive energy. Neither Capricorn nor Scorpio go in for great shows of affection at the drop of a hat but make no mis-take, little Scorpio needs constant reassurance to keep big emotions in balance. Great strength hides extremely sensi-tive inner feelings that

need encouragement in expressing themselves. Extreme by nature, black/white, saint/sinner, a powerhouse of enthusiasm or a plethora of self-indulgent laziness. Take your pick. Good firm guidance and plenty of affection can put this born winner on the right road. You both share a strong ambitious streak but each approaches this in a different way. You work steadily a little at a time toward your aims; little Scorpio leaves everything to the last minute until all looks impossible and then sets to, overcomes against all odds and wins! You'd hate it but with this little one it always seems to work. Life is rarely dull with a little Scorpio about!

...and now the bad news!

If you play strong and fair with Junior the loyalty will be unbounded, but unbending and stingy nit-picking can cause a resentful rift in the relationship that may never be bridged. Yes, even the old Goat can be a nag! When the 'You shoulds' begin to dominate the relationship little Scorpio will shut down all communications and you'll know what they mean by Secretive Scorpio. Remember this little extremist loves or hates, nothing in the middle. Best to quietly admire the achievements rather than pointing out where there could be improvements. Scorpios are highly self-critical and always know where they can better themselves. Leave it to the Scorpion and stay happy.

THE AQUARIUS PARENT

The good news!

You don't follow the crowd, do what others do because of what the neighbours think. You approach everything with a new eye and a spirit of adventure. Lucky little Scorpio! You are bound to have a few original or avant-garde tricks up the sleeve when it comes to bringing up children. 'What was good enough for my parents is good enough for me' may suit some, but the Aquarian, never! Open to anything extreme or challenging, little Scorpio will find great stimulation and fun with this unusual parent. Both find enormous interest in other people, Junior through a natural intuitive understanding of what others are thinking and feeling, while the parent just loves people for themselves, and listens. The dialogue and succession of visitors can be perpetual. Scorpios' extreme nature, without some limitations in the form of well adhered to guidelines, will lead them to experiment at both ends of any scale. Doing nothing by halves, they can be saints or sinners;

with no limits they'll try the lot. Much as rules and regulations go against the grain with Aquarians, they are a positive must if you want Junior to hit the peaks rather than the depths. The penetrating mind of this intense and enthusiastic youngster will respond well to the individual theories and ideals of the Aquarian parent. Strong and often extremely self-possessed outwardly, Scorpions need plenty of demonstrative affection to feel really secure; they're tough enough to do without it but why should they? Nobody is ever going to know what dramas are enacted internally by a love-deprived, secretive, keep-it-to-oneself, Scorpion. Give them a hug as often as you can.

...and now the bad news!

The Aquarian world is viewed through the mind, highly intelligent, logical; it would not be surprising if little Scorpio, with her quick mental responses, was seen as having the same kind of drive. Not so! Little Scorpio sees the world through feelings with an almost psychic 'tuning in' to anything that takes the attention. If this passionate and completely involved little child reads this parent's detachment as not caring there can be bottled up resentment. Both drives are essential but difficult for the other to understand. Somehow, when difficulties occur, you will have to bridge the gap between your forward-looking and your little one's more traditional approach.

THE PISCES PARENT

The good news!

You gentle Pisceans rarely forget the strong images of your own childhood, and sympathetically and sensitively understand the hopes, fears, strengths, and weaknesses of any of your little charges. Young Scorpio's strong-feeling nature will find warmth and security with this caring Pisces parent. Though highly sensitive, the concentrated power that emanates from these little Scorpions can be bewildering. Extremes of action seem to be the rule: overwork or laziness, absolute crazes or emphatic hates, everything in life black or white, but never grey. A great deal of help from the Piscean imagination will go a long way in putting up more worthwhile challenges for this youngster to defeat. Though seeming quite confident and self-possessed from an early age, the little Scorpio is quite prepared to hide any deep hurts and emotional insecurities with hardly a clue given. Pisces' almost psychic awareness will sense these and give constant caring support. This will go a long way towards helping but will never stop this youngster from needing to experience and internalise the extremes of emotion. Little Scorpios need to live life intensely and to the full, and this will include the worst temptations you can imagine, so some pretty good

guidelines will have to be drawn. As both of you are strongly sensitive and driven by your feelings there should be an almost psychic rapport that may find you each saying what the other was thinking. Both of you share a love of creative imagination and you would do well to share plenty of creative activities for your mutual pleasure. Often little Scorpios are talented in several directions and filling the home with stimulating material could bring surprising results. It is amazing how many houses are full of gadgets that provide entertainment and yet are devoid of materials for making and doing things oneself.

...and now the bad news!

Pisceans tend to idealise their loved ones as a whole but especially their children. For this reason they can be almost lax when it comes to discipline and in this relationship that can spell disaster. If little Scorpio is testing out his strength and finding out just how far he can go, how disconcerting when the fences are continually moved further and further away. Pisceans are often over-indulgent and an easy touch where their darling babes are concerned. Little Scorpio can become a little horror in this climate, exploiting Ma or Pa for all they're worth. If you want to produce a nasty Scorpio, introduce one to the gentle art of manipulating others for their own gain. They take to it like a cat to mousing! Come on Pisces, stand firm, your little one needs better things to do.

On the Cusp

Many people whose children are born on the day the sun changes signs are not sure whether they come under one sign or another. Some say one is supposed to be a little bit of each but this is rarely true. Adjoining signs are very different to each other so checking up can make everything clear. The opposite table gives the exact Greenwich Mean Time (GMT) when the sun moves into Scorpio and when it leaves. Subtract or add the hours indicated below for your nearest big city.

AMSTERDAM	GMT + 01.00	MADRID	GMT + 01.00
ATHENS	GMT + 02.00	MELBOURNE	GMT + 10.00
BOMBAY	GMT + 05.30	MONTREAL	GMT - 05.00
CAIRO	GMT + 02.00	NEW YORK	GMT - 05.00
CALGARY	GMT - 07.00	PARIS	GMT + 01.00
CHICAGO	GMT - 06.00	ROME	GMT + 01.00
DURBAN	GMT + 02.00	S.FRANCISCO	GMT - 08.00
GIBRALTAR	GMT + 01.00	SYDNEY	GMT + 10.00
HOUSTON	GMT - 06.00	TOKYO	GMT + 09.00
LONDON	GMT 00.00	WELLINGTON	GMT + 12.00

DATE	ENTERS SCORPIO	GMT	LEAVES SCORPIO	GMT
1984	OCT 23	5.46 AM	NOV 22	3.11 AM
1985	OCT 23	11.22 AM	NOV 22	8.51 AM
1986	OCT 23	5.14 PM	NOV 22	2.45 PM
1987	OCT 23	11.01 PM	NOV 22	8.30 PM
1988	OCT 23	4.45 AM	NOV 22	2.12 AM
1989	OCT 23	10.35 AM	NOV 22	8.05 AM
1990	OCT 23	4.14 PM	NOV 22	1.47 PM
1991	OCT 23	10.05 PM	NOV 22	7.36 PM
1992	OCT 23	3.57 AM	NOV 22	1.26 AM
1993	OCT 23	9.37 AM	NOV 22	7.07 AM
1994	OCT 23	3.36 PM	NOV 22	1.06 PM
1995	OCT 23	9.32 PM	NOV 22	7.02 PM
1996	OCT 23	3.19 AM	NOV 22	12.50 AM
1997	OCT 23	9.15 AM	NOV 22	6.48 AM
1998	OCT 23	2.59 PM	NOV 22	12.35 PM
1999	OCT 23	8.53 PM	NOV 22	6.25 PM
2000	OCT 23	2.48 AM	NOV 22	12.20 AM
2001	OCT 23	8.26 AM	NOV 22	6.01 AM
2002	OCT 23	2.18 PM	NOV 22	11.54 AM
2003	OCT 23	8.09 PM	NOV 22	5.44 PM
2004	OCT 23	1.50 AM	NOV 21	11.23 PM